Contents

Words appearing in the text in bold, **like this**, are explained in the Glossary.

 Find out more about Nature's Patterns at www.heinemannexplore.co.uk

Nature's patterns

Nature is always changing. Many of the changes that happen follow a **pattern**. This means that they happen over and over again.

Giraffes use their long necks to reach leaves to eat.

Food Chains

Anita Ganeri

Heinemann
LIBRARY

Young
Explorer

www.heinemann.co.uk/library
Visit our website to find out more information about **Heinemann Library** books.

To order:
☎ Phone 44 (0) 1865 888066
🖷 Send a fax to 44 (0) 1865 314091
🖳 Visit the Heinemann Bookshop at www.heinemann.co.uk/library to browse our catalogue and order online.

First published in Great Britain by Heinemann Library, Halley Court, Jordan Hill, Oxford OX2 8EJ, part of Harcourt Education. Heinemann is a registered trademark of Harcourt Education Ltd.

Editorial: Jilly Attwood, Kate Bellamy
Design: Jo Hinton-Malivoire
Picture research: Ginny Stroud-Lewis, Ruth Blair
Production: Séverine Ribierre

Originated by Ambassador Litho Ltd
Printed and bound in China by South China Printing Company

ISBN 978 0 431 11396 8 (hardback)
08 07 06 05 04
10 9 8 7 6 5 4 3 2 1

ISBN 978 0 431 11402 6 (paperback)
09 08
10 9 8 7 6 5 4 3 2

British Library Cataloguing in Publication Data
Ganeri, Anita
Food Chains - (Nature's Patterns)
577.1'6
A full catalogue record for this book is available from the British Library.

Acknowledgements
The Publishers would like to thank the following for permission to reproduce photographs: Corbis pp. **23** (David Aubrey), **6** (Gaetano), **4**, **19** (Royalty Free); Digital Vision pp. **26**, **27**; Getty Images/Photodisc p. **8** [soil], **9**, **20**; Heather Angel pp. **5**, **21** (Natural Visions); NHPA p. **16**; NHPA pp. **24** (Laurie Campbell), **14** (Darek Karp), **22** (Haroldo Palo Jr), **13** (Roy Waller); Nature Photo Library pp. **10**, **12**, **15**, **17**, **25**, **29**; Science Photo Library p. **11**, **18**; Tudor Photography p. **8** [flower].

Cover photograph of a koala is reproduced with permission of Nature Photo Library.

Our thanks to David Lewin for his assistance in the preparation of this book.

Every effort has been made to contact copyright holders of any material reproduced in this book. omissions will be rectified in subsequent printings if notice is given to the Publishers.

The paper used to print this book comes from sustainable resources.

This eagle uses its sharp claws to catch fish to eat.

All animals need to eat to stay alive. Animals are linked together in a pattern by the things they eat.

food Chains

Plants and animals are linked by the food they need. This **pattern** is called a **food chain**. Each plant or animal is a link in the chain.

All living things are part of a food chain, including you.

Each link in the food chain is eaten by the next in line. Some food chains are very simple, like the one below.

Plants are eaten by rabbits. In turn, owls eat the rabbits.

grasses and seeds　　　　rabbit　　　　owl

Plants for starters

Most **food chains** start off with green plants. The plants are the first link in the food chain. This is because plants can make food from sunlight.

sunlight energy

water taken up by roots

This butterfly feeds on **nectar** from inside a flower.

Animals cannot make their own food. They have to move about and find things to eat. Some animals eat plants. Some animals eat other animals.

Plant-eaters

Some animals only eat plants. After plants, these animals are the next link in the **food chain**. They are called **herbivores**, which means plant-eaters.

Caterpillars are herbivores. They eat leaves.

This animal is a **crustacean**. It lives in the sea and eats water plants.

Some herbivores eat leaves or grass. Some eat fruit, nuts and seeds. Others suck juices from plant stems. Some munch underwater plants.

Meat-eaters

Some animals like to eat **herbivores**. These animals are the next link in the **food chain**. They are called **carnivores**, which means meat-eaters.

Birds eat caterpillars and feed them to their chicks.

Ringed seals eat **crustaceans**. They crush them with their strong teeth.

Carnivores have special tools for catching their food. Lions and wolves have sharp, pointed teeth. Eagles have hooked beaks and large claws, called talons.

Eating plants and animals

Many animals have a mixed **diet**. They eat different kinds of plants and animals. These animals are called **omnivores**.

Large birds like this sparrowhawk eat smaller birds.

Bears, foxes, raccoons and people are all omnivores. Raccoons eat fruit, eggs, worms and insects. Many people eat fruit, vegetables, meat and fish.

Polar bears hunt for seals on the ice. They also eat seaweed.

Using up waste

In nature, everything is used again. After a plant or animal dies, its body starts to rot. **Fungi**, worms and **bacteria** feed on the dead body.

Worms, fungi and bacteria are all called **decomposers**.

Nutrients from dead plants and animals soak into the soil. This makes the soil rich, so plants can grow. Animals eat the plants and the **food chain** starts again.

Most fungi live on dead plants and animals.

In the sea

Food chains happen everywhere. In the sea, there are many different food chains. But they all start with tiny plants called plant plankton.

Sharks have sharp teeth for eating meat.

Tiny animals nibble at the plants. Then fish and larger animals eat the smaller ones. This happens again and again along the food chain.

fresh water

Fresh water is not salty like sea water. It is found in rivers, lakes and ponds. Each of these places has its own **food chains**.

Water plants are food for snails, fish and other animals.

In one kind of river food chain, snails eat water plants. Then fish eat the snails. In turn, a heron catches the fish to eat.

In the rainforest

It is hot and steamy in the rainforest. Plants grow quickly in the warmth. Millions of animals live among the plants and need them for food.

In the rainforest there are lots of plants for insects to eat.

Insects make tasty snacks for tree frogs.

In one rainforest **food chain**, insects eat the juicy leaves of trees. Tree frogs eat the insects. Then snakes and birds eat the tree frogs.

In the woods

Woodland plants and trees are tasty stores of food for animals. Their leaves, flowers, bark, fruit, nuts, stems and roots can all be eaten.

Squirrels eat nuts which are full of goodness.

Bats fly about at night to find moths to eat.

Some woodland animals come out to find food at night. Moths drink flower **nectar**. Bats fly after the moths and catch them in mid-air.

Desert diets

The dry, dusty desert is a difficult place to live. Plants and animals have to be tough. There is very little to eat and drink.

Camels can go for weeks without drinking. They get some water by eating desert plants.

Desert plants and seeds store water. Insects, such as locusts and crickets, eat the desert plants. Then, lizards and scorpions munch on the juicy insects.

This desert lizard is looking for insects to eat.

food webs

An animal may eat a mixture of things. It can be a **link** in many different **food chains**. These food chains join up to make a food web.

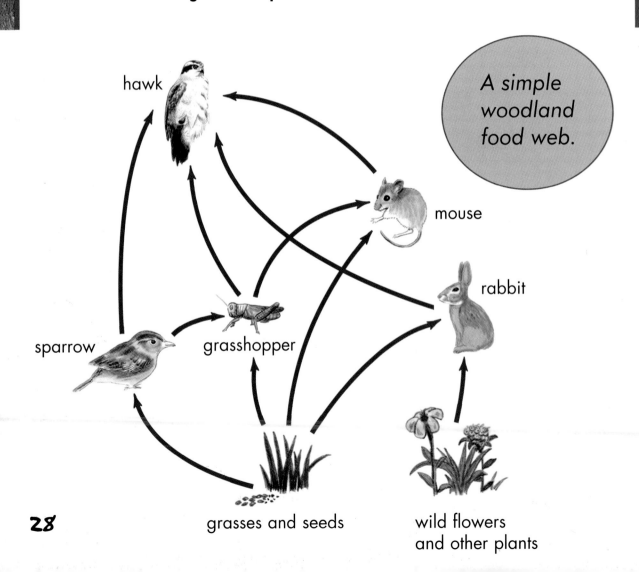

hawk

A simple woodland food web.

mouse

rabbit

sparrow

grasshopper

grasses and seeds

wild flowers and other plants

In the Arctic, foxes feed on birds that eat fish. The fish eat tiny sea animals. These tiny animals are also eaten by huge whales.

The Arctic fox catches birds to eat.

Pyramid of numbers

In a **food chain**, there are usually more plants than **herbivores**. There are more herbivores than **carnivores** or **omnivores**.

Drawing a pyramid can show the numbers of living things in a food chain. In this pyramid, there is more grass than rabbits, and more rabbits than owls.

  Find out more about Nature's Patterns at <u>www.heinemannexplore.co.uk</u>

Glossary

bacteria tiny living things

carnivores animals that eat other animals

crustacean animals such as shrimps, prawns and crabs

decomposers living things that break down dead plants and animals

food chain the way plants and animals are linked by food

fungi type of living things, like mushrooms and toadstools

herbivores animals that eat plants

nectar sweet syrup inside flowers

nutrients chemicals made by plants and animals that help them grow

omnivores animals that eat plants and animals

pattern something that happens over and over again

More books to read

Cycles in Nature: Food Chains, Theresa Greenaway (Hodder, 2001)

Usborne Internet Linked Pocket Science: Why do people eat?, Kate Needham (Usborne Publishing, 2001)

Index